All I See Is You

Jessica Urlichs

Contents

Motherhood has broken me, healed me,
and humbled me all at once.

Just You Wait and See

'Just you wait and see'.

You'll hear those words a bit mama, in fact you probably already have.
You'll be reminded that if you think you're tired now,
'Just you wait and see'.

If you think you're sore now,
'Just you wait and see'.

If you think you're busy now,
'Just you wait and see'.

There's so much you'll be told and a lot of it is true,
but there's so much they don't say too.

They'll tell you the birth is painful, but did they tell you about
your strength? The strength you always had that could bring a life
into this world and shortly after leave you breathless?

They'll tell you it's the most rewarding job in the world, but did
they tell you they felt lonely some days? That some days a rain
cloud followed them around and they mourned for more than
dishes, washing and burp cloths. You'll wonder how this can be
so hard when loving them comes so easy?

They'll tell you that you'll lose yourself in motherhood, but did
they tell you to stop looking for her? It's still you, just a new
version, reborn as a mother.

She is coming to find you, so stand still for a moment.

They'll tell you of how fast they grow and it's true. One minute you're their whole world, the next they're venturing down the hallway and room by room it becomes bigger. It's sad when they leave versions of themselves behind, but be proud mama, they're going places!

They'll tell you they hope you have a good baby, one who sleeps through the night, maybe you'll be lucky? But did they tell you to just surrender? The pain of fatigue is haunting but they need you right now. It's not because you didn't follow some schedule, it's because you're their home, they are all good babies.

They'll tell you about the worry and the guilt, how some days it'll consume you. But did they tell you mum guilt seeks out the good mums? The ones who have so much love they are winded by it? Mum guilt will lie to you, so remember, you are enough, you are more than enough.

They'll tell you about that first smile, about how precious that moment would be. But did they tell you it happens when you need it the most? The fourth trimester can be tough, but almost as if planned that smile will save you.

They'll tell you it's a strain on your relationship and it can be, it's not easy. But did they tell you that it won't always be this way? One day you'll have your nights back again, the house will be clean and the rooms will be silent and your heart will be in pieces because of it.

It's a beautiful bumpy road where the best isn't just yet to come.
The best is yesterday, today and tomorrow.
That's motherhood.
And it's magic.
Just you wait and see.

Darling Dreamer

Darling dreamer, if only you knew
There's many more colours
Than the playground you knew
Of the swings that met stars
In red, yellow and blue.
Now apricot sunrise
Or quiet dark shadows.
Don't open those eyes
To be met with arrows.
All children of mothers
Can feel small too
With trembling limbs
So perfectly new
And so perfectly made.
I hope you don't listen
When they say,
What you're not
What you are
What you're given.
Those hands will grow
As magic is made.
It's all so new
And I know you're afraid.
Darling dreamer,
Your dream has come true
It can be in your arms
As you dream for more too.
If only you knew,
Mama, these words are for you.

Blink and You'll Miss It

'Blink and you'll miss it', they say.
But I didn't miss it, I was there.

I was there, placing you down to sleep on your back, elbows in line with your shoulders, hands at your ears.
I always wondered why tiny babies slept that way.
Then you rolled over, then you were sitting, and now you're jumping from the coffee table to the couch.

I was there, through the tears of breastfeeding, pinching my leg or curling my toes. I wondered if I could do this again. Then one day we were in the kitchen, I was stirring dinner and you were feeding in my other arm, and I smiled, how did we get here?

I was there, pacing the hallway, squinting my eyes shut, wishing the moment away. Shattered beyond measure at the thought of another day on no sleep. I was there as you cuddled into me, as we surrendered to each other. I still envelop you into my arms, but you don't fold into me the same and you tell me when you're ready for your cot now.

I was there, as they placed you on my chest, never more alive, never more terrified. My world in my arms as I listened to those tiny squawks. Now you're saying things like, 'I don't want to', 'I love you' or 'Go 'way Mummy'.

I don't remember when the nights got easier but they did, or when you stopped saying "uggle" instead of cuddle, or the

moment I kissed those little feet and was greeted with sweat instead of your signature newborn scent.
Oh, how I know I will miss this when I look back through the rear-view mirror.

How I know, that no matter how testing, memory lane will be tree lined with nostalgia.
Will I truly remember it as it was?
Or will I be trying to pin down a bubble?

When do all the becoming's become going's or gone's?

'Blink and you'll miss it', they say.

But we don't miss it.
We miss saying goodbye to it.

Alone Time

Her face is painted,
less hair on her body.
She felt more beautiful at home she realised,
but she was here now.
She had forgotten the sound of silence,
though there's never a silent moment in her head.
She keeps a treasure chest of splashes of bath water,
shrieks of delight,
'Mummy's' and
'I love you's'.
Touches of tiny hands and buries the yelling
and tears under the colours, and other various things.
She can't rest her puppet string bones
even though she wants to.
To unmarry what is needed of her skin.
Just for a night so the weight can fall off.
But her mother heart feels empty from the stretch.
Even though she could close her eyes, they stay open.
She wonders what they're doing.
She knows now mothers are never alone.
Even when they are.

How Far Away Are You?

What I say
How far away are you?
I'm tired
I told you, remember?
Don't forget to pack XYZ
Why didn't you pack XYZ?
I don't know, you decide
No
You just don't get it
Can you imagine when…
Do you remember when…
Are you serious?
YOU try doing this all day
Not tonight babe
Why didn't you cry at the birth?
I can't do it all
Here, let me
Who are we?
Can I just have ONE moment!

What I mean
I miss you a bit
You're a really good Dad
How far away are you?

Dear Friend

Dear Friend,

It's still me,

Well sort of.

I'm here, but another version entirely.

I'm in a bubble of longing and love.

I know you messaged me this morning, or was it yesterday?
It's all a bit of a blur and my phones buried somewhere on my
bedside that has never felt so small.

I so badly want to reconnect with you but I'm trying to
reconnect with me too.

I'm cancelling a lot and it's hard to say why; the anxiety has held
me prisoner here a bit and I want to talk about nothing, and
everything. I want to pour a wine and laugh with you. But I don't
know how to be the girl of yesterday.

I also want to try and get some sleep, but even when I'm able to
I'm scrolling through photos or checking if he's breathing in his
cot.

I've never had such fulfilment, but I feel a bit empty right now,
even though the room is full, even though my heart is too.

I'm still accepting that my milestones now are first smiles, the way he now looks at me in true focus; I told my husband he must definitely know I'm his mother by now.
I wonder if there will be anything else I can talk about.
I think some days I'm still truly waiting for all this to hit me.

I'm a mother now.

My nights aren't popping bottles; they're pouring milk into them or figuring out the latch. I'm trying to find time to eat a full meal, or shower. Can you believe I plan that stuff now?
I'm not waking up with a hangover and texting you straight away about last night's antics. I still feel hungover, but I'm not the one who's been drinking all night.

My bones ache, my heart aches and I also have a headache, I think from this constant mum bun my hair lives in.

I'm not sure I can hold it all together. I know I don't have to with you, but right now I just need to try.

This is my life right now, nap schedules, dressing gowns at 2pm, google searches, doctor's appointments and a constant reminder that my phone storage is full.
It's hard to swallow but I want to inhale it all.

Oh it's a whirlwind Friend, but one I'm glad to be caught up in.
Please keep checking in.
Please keep inviting me.
It means more than you know.

I'll be back.
In some shape or form.

A Little Messy

Sometimes it feels like my patience is wearing thin. I can feel it bubbling up inside me, one more scream from one of them and I'll probably scream back.

I remind myself about pulling myself back to the present, enjoying each and every moment. I can hear them yelling for me, I can hear the million things swirling round in my head. The push and pull of being present and being 5 steps ahead too. Sometimes I just need to go to another place entirely to deal with being present.

I think about self-care, me the empty shelf just waiting to be restocked. In this season of being so needed I wonder if we should talk about self-care being blasting music in the car on the way to supermarket or getting through an episode of a series before one of them wakes. It's not retreats and face masks for all of us, not quite yet.

Sometimes when my husband walks in from work, I can see he's already recognised my expression to know what kind of day I've had. I want to shrug off his embrace as if it's his fault, that knee jerk silly resentment. Even though I wouldn't change it, even though I've never been more rewarded in my life. Even though I appreciate him immensely.

It's taken me a long time to lower the bar, a long time to count two simultaneous naps as an achievement. It's taken a long time because I'm hard on myself, maybe we all are.
Motherhood reignited a flame within me, yes, but on those

harder days it feels like there's no oxygen and the flame is struggling.

It's not the mess that bothers me.
It's the mess in my head.

I think we forget to talk about that sometimes.

Maybe because we think it makes us seem ungrateful?

Maybe because we are still yet to truly place value on the work we are doing at home raising these tiny humans?
Maybe because we compare ourselves to others and forget their mess is swept out of the frame?

We're all going through it in some way or another.

Cup's overflowing with love.
Cup's depleted.
Cup's sitting stagnant in the microwave.

We're all a little tired, a little lost, a little messy.

Nocturnal Mother

Let's lie with the moon
our familiar friend
let's cradle up in darkness
as our eyes adjust again
let's breathe each other in
let's grow
let's sway
let's fall to pieces
let's grow again
let's sweep up the stardust
let's wake up the sun
let the new day pour in
a clean slate has begun
my heart tells my bones
it is beautiful
it is ours
yet I daydream for sleep
as my eyes begin to weep.

Not Every Day Is Beautiful

Not every day is beautiful
But you are
I can't wait for some days to end
But you're my beginning
My middle
My meeting place
Some moments I just want to be alone
Even though every moment with you is perfect
It doesn't always feel like that though
Not in that moment
When plans fall over
When no one sleeps
When I'm overwhelmed
You may deplete me some days
But you complete me every day
You're the bags under my eyes at all hours of the night
My tears of fatigue
You're also
My heart
My breath
You're the ground that brings me to my knees
The ground you walk on I adore
My grounding
You're my weakness
And the strength that I need

The build-up
The break-down
My vulnerability
You are the tune I hum
My scream
My follow
My fall
My finding
The broth of my bones
My skin
My thoughts before and after
You are mine but not mine to keep
But you keep all of me
Even though I ache
Even though some days are so very hard
Even though I doubt I'm doing this right
Not every moment is beautiful
But you are
You are the promise of love in a tired storm
Even though I may wish some moments away
You're the hands of the clock I will to stand still
And I am at the hands of you.

Deep Feelings

My boy from such a young age has had this innate capacity to feel, really feel.

One that we all have deep within us, only his comes with questions, ones that linger far beyond the moments. Tears that come purely from how others are feeling.

His highly sensitive nature has been a beautiful blessing but has caused me plenty of challenging questions also. Ones where I have had to look deep within myself and ask why I'm challenged by his reactions, probably because I have always felt so deeply too.

In the past I remember conversations with others, they would laugh over a situation that had happened to someone else, meanwhile I've already transported myself into that persons shoes, crushed by the weight of something I don't necessarily have a connection to, but I'm carrying the feelings as if they're my own.
I've been told to lighten up in the past, that's a hard thing to hear when you have an incredible light within you but it gets dulled by statements like that.

I know who Harry is and I know why it triggers me sometimes, because we're so alike. His nature is so close to mine. I spent a long time suppressing it, thinking that maybe I was too much, I felt TOO MUCH.

He feels music before he hears it.

He will watch a cartoon where a dog might fall over and he will cry and ask if the doggy was OK, again before he goes to bed at night.

He can pick up on the vibe in a room in seconds and recognises big feelings in others.

Loud noises will rock him to his core while my daughter doesn't bat an eyelid. I can feel myself squinting. Is it because of his reaction, or because I feel it too?

My goal that I must succeed in with him is to never make him feel uncomfortable for these feelings, or that it's something to simply 'get over' but instead accept and get through.

The world needs more of our highly sensitive children, ones who lead with their heart.
They are critical to this world, not a burden.

And through him I'm realising I didn't need all the answers, just acceptance.

My Season

My darling,
You were the storm that crashed against me
and took the shoreline with it.
The tide that rocked and soothed me.
The wind that had me mourning for the leaves you
kissed into autumn.
You were the fire that ignited mine when the darkness
took hold.
The sun showers that moved me in streams down my cheeks.
The warmth that breathed life into my core.
My roots grounded.
My heart soaring.
You were the seasons they spoke of.
Ever changing and blooming.
For I thought I was growing you,
When you were growing me too.

Enjoy Every Minute

'Enjoy every minute',

says the twinkle of their eye in a sea of calm.

The storm has long passed.

But they've been here before.

So says the lines on their face

and the body that's been and birthed and bore.

They read from pages past,

from tiny chapters of nostalgia.

I listen smiling,

with ringing ears from echoed woes,

as they round and round the garden,

'look at those tiny toes'.

Time to do the dishes, or washing,

or some quick task I think.

Phrases must come so easy

once all has been written.

Maybe it's different when you're in it.

Can you still be utterly in love

and not enjoy every minute?

New Streets

I drive down streets I've never seen before while they sleep.
I've lived here my whole life, but I've missed the avenues veins.
I'm tired, and meanwhile the world convinces me that I should
be doing more.
But I need the silence, I need these unfamiliar streets.
I need to continue a thought, and right now I can.

Like how we pick apart the bones of a mother until we collapse
under the weight of it all. I keep driving. They keep sleeping.

Like how we don't talk about the loneliness sometimes, how the
vines of it thicken around our days.

Like how my head is above water now, but somehow I'm busier
than ever, a type of busy I would never change, except I would
wash my hair more. Just sleep a little longer.

Like how songs are time machines and I hope their eyes will be
the notes of my memories.

Like how this is living, we don't start again tomorrow, each
moment belongs, even this one. The rain comes.

I realise when I drive, the rear-view mirror is always tilted so I
can still see their faces slightly.

Like every thought, I see them, every decision, I see them.
My reflection, them.

We head towards home.

I smile as one of them opens their eyes.
I smile because I'm a little more whole again.
I smile because even as they sleep, they show me things I've
never seen.
Even if today it's just overgrown lawns down new streets.

Motherhood's Contradiction

I've been the happiest since I've had children.
I've also been at my lowest.

I'm a much better version of myself.
I also haven't always liked what I've seen when mirrors have
been held up to me.

I've never been in more company.
And at times never felt so lonely.

Some days I don't want to end.
Some days I wish away, oh and the guilt from feeling that when
they grow so fast.

I've never been so sure of who I'm meant to be.
I've never wondered so much who I am.

I've never felt closer with my husband.
But at times, I've never felt more distant.

I believe in myself, I trust myself.
I've questioned myself and doubted myself.

I always want to be better for them.
But I've yelled and cried and wished I'd handled certain
situations better.

I've never loved so hard and so fiercely.
And I've never felt so vulnerable.

I've never been more broken.
And I've never been more complete.

I've never smiled so much.
I've never cried so much.

I've never craved alone time more.
But when I am I always feel like something's missing, like an arm.

I've never been so excited to watch them grow.
And simultaneously wished they'd stay little forever.

Some days I feel like I've achieved nothing.
But as I think of them at night, I know I've achieved everything.

I've never looked forward to so much.
And I've also, never looked back.

It's one beautiful contradiction.
A journey of wrong turns that are probably still right.
And dreams of the future even if you don't get enough sleep to dream.
Exhaustion but effortless love.
The hardest and most rewarding thing ever.
Motherhood.

That Silly Crane

I had a moment of realisation yesterday,
my little boy squeals a lot, mostly when he's excited about
something but also when he doesn't like something. What's on
TV, Holly playing with his toys, what's for dinner. Whatever he's
trying to say comes out in a squeal that sounds like a pterodactyl.
I started responding with 'Harry, I can't understand you when
you squeal'. I would wait for him to speak in a calmer tone and
then I'd respond calmly back to what he was wanting.

Then yesterday we were in the car, and he spotted a crane
outside the window. He squealed so loudly, 'LOOK MUMMY A
CRANE', I didn't even think and I responded, 'don't squeal,
Harry'. He then said back calmly, 'Look Mummy... a crane', no
excitement and in a tone that didn't belong to a two year old.
I felt completely crushed and instantly filled with regret. My eyes
started to sting as I looked at him in the rear-view mirror looking
out to the construction, deflated.

It gave me one of those heart twinges, suddenly I realised how
beautiful that excited squeal was. I was trying to grab it back in
my mind as if it were too late.
I hated myself in that moment, for being responsible for him
growing faster than he should.

Those rush of emotions are all part of growing, all valid, all
perfect.
The drive home was a sad one, for me, for him and maybe for
the silly crane that stood there in its spot waiting for
little fingers to point at it.

This morning he spotted something out the window in the car and his voice went up a few octaves, he went to correct it and I joined in with his excitement instead. I've never been happier to hear his little squeal return, this time about a yellow digger... 'and all those rocks Mummy, LOOK MUMMY, LOOK!'

My First Love

There will be memories we make that will be filled with laughter but also ones soaked in tears.
I used to tell you everything, but it feels like we haven't talked in days, swept away in the seasons of babies and toddler-hood.
Finding ourselves again, sewing up the past and unpicking bits of ourselves with it.

I sometimes wonder who we are now.

How would your hands feel if not for holding our sons?
What of my chest if not for the comfort of our daughter?

They are an extension of our love and our love for them is so great there's almost a pain in surrendering to that.
A gentle shift that leaves us cracked open.
I couldn't be closer to you, and I couldn't miss you more.

It's been years of happiness and fatigue.
Years of fulfillment and empty vases.
How do we move forward if we're trying to find our way back?
In some ways, like them, we're brand new.

I draw in a breath that feels heavier as it reaches my eyes.
Despite those free-range moments where routine is thrown to the wind.
There's still a ladder in my throat and I can't climb out.

While they are every inch of my breath, you are still my first love.

All I See Is You

Mama,

I can't see past you right now, I'm so small and everything's a little blurry.

All I see is you.

When you feel alone, like the walls are closing in, remember I'm here too. I know your world has changed and the days feel a little lonely. But they aren't lonely for me.

You are my everything.

When you feel like you don't know what you're doing, you're making it look easy to me. Even though we're still getting to know each other, you know me better than anyone.

I trust you.

When you think some nights you'll never sleep again, you will. We both will. But I'm scared right now. I promise I'm not manipulating you. I just need your smell and comfort. Do you feel that tug in your heart when we're apart? I do too.

I miss you.

When you feel as if you've achieved nothing, please know, my cup has never been so full. The days that get away from you will be some of my best memories of us playing together on the ground.

I love you.

When you feel like you don't know who you are anymore, when you turn away from the mirror. That face will be the one I look to when I achieve something, the one I search for in a crowd. The reason for my first smile.

You're perfect to me.

When you feel like the weight of it all is heavy in your heart, please know I've never felt lighter. Can I lay here with you a little longer? I won't always need you like this.

But I need you right now.

When you feel as if you have nothing left to give, when I see your hands outstretched at me, pleading. When we're both crying. I wish I could talk, but I can't. If I could, I would tell you,

There's a reason I chose you.

I can't see past you right now mama, because you are my world. It will get bigger, soon enough.

But for now,

All I see is you.

It's All A Bit Quick

Sometimes I stare at you and already see the outline of the man you're going to be.Each beautiful and challenging version of you filling those spaces.

It's all getting a bit quick.
All of a sudden I don't know if those curls will return.
Your legs even hang over the couch a bit now.
The baby swing at the park seems awkward.

I want to remember all of you, because I'm so worried I'll forget.
I'm so quick to wipe away those hand prints on the window.
So quick to hurry you when you're collecting rocks on our walk.
So quick.
Even your expressions are getting older, they don't catch you by surprise anymore. Some are learnt, even borrowed.

I've wished away hard days and I hate that I've wished away anything with you in it.
Is this how motherhood works?
Be still my heart, but get me through?

It's 3am and I'm carving out your face in my mind, even though it's dark and the light creeping under the door is calling.
As I reach it I hear a soft, "Mummy come back".
Oh, the irony that one day all I'll wish for is for you to come back to me.

'Don't worry, it won't always be this way', is on repeat in my head.
Maybe never a truer word has been said.

Our Heartbeats

My daughter still loves listening to my heartbeat. Every night before bed we sit there together on our chair in her room as she happily drifts off. I can't be wearing a robe or anything over my chest, she fusses until there's skin to skin.

She puts her nose on my chest and breathes in and makes a melody of calm. I always go with it because natures so beautiful like that. It teaches us about how we were always enough. Especially on those days I feel like I'm not even close, I'm reminded that this closeness IS enough.

I think of the comments of it being habitual, of the time I can't get back being spent in her room. It's true, this might become habitual, she might seek comfort by climbing onto my lap later or crying into my neck when she's older telling me of her troubles.
And I won't get this time back, that's true too.
Because one day she will stop.
And one day I'll miss her even though she's right there.
And that one day will be a today.
They are long and they are short but these memories we are making through whispers in our skin is the warmth she will always feel.
As independence in her grows, there will be less room for me.
Because this will be over in a heartbeat.
But the memories will be carried in them forever.

Rubbish Day

These days a bed with us both
doesn't need a baby between
for us to be separate
or feel unseen
a thought of you is quickly replaced
about them, or the chores
or shrugging off your embrace
never far from apart
as you pull me in close
a beautiful battle
of who needs me the most
my energy drained bit by bit
my arms pulled to elastic
my hair fraying like a ragdoll
what to do with your compliments
when my reflection's so fragile
it's not your fault
you see me the same
mum, mummy, babe, honey
I've forgotten my name
my heart is so full yet it's still healing
I open my mouth and speak
words with no feeling
we talk when it's dark and all is done
once the trials from the day
are razor sharp on my tongue
and to extend further warmth
just feels like a chore

there's no pictures of just us
on my phone anymore
it's not that I don't love you, I do
more than ever
it's the ships we've become
drifting off in the weather
and I long to fall into those arms
so much
but I don't quite know what to do
with your touch
I know beautiful and ragged
become one and the same
when we speak of mothers
when we speak of this change.
it shouldn't be such an effort should it?
to be a mother, a wife, a lover
and everything I was before and after
I love how you try
with all of your strength
to break down my walls
while my arm holds our length
it's all I imagined
bum pats over dishes
while our babes are tucked up
it's not perfect, yet it is
I watched you with the kids the other night
it felt warm in my chest
everything felt right
I smiled
tell him
TELL HIM
you looked up
and I swallowed
'are you taking out the bins?'

Today I Met My Match

Today I met my match.
Toddlers.
I've never been a cryer, but ohhh motherhood has got me GOOD!

A lot of mornings I wake up already too tired to leap into the routine ahead. But I do it, minus the leaping.

I worry a lot, I carry the worlds weight on my shoulders, I worry so much about my kids, I worry we should be doing more, what, I don't really know.
At night I'm either falling asleep or wanting to stay up just to enjoy a moment of gathering thoughts or thinking about nothing, I'd take either.

The newborn stage is hard, we talk about the fourth trimester but the toddler stage is TESTING. The juggling of care whilst working, getting yourself back into a rhythm of the old but new you.
Discovering, constant discovering.
These toddler years, as beautiful as they are, can be like looking at a miniature version of yourself and wanting to yell at them while simultaneously wanting to hug them.
In some ways it feels like I don't have the right to still be so tearful, I've got amazing support and the maternity leave period is over now, so 'you'll be right'.
But the overwhelm is still there, it's a whole bunch of things but when you finally untangle it, they're just little jobs and thoughts that have piled up.

It was all beginning to feel a little thankless today, there was fighting, yelling, food throwing, I was picking up toys and sighing to hold back tears when I felt a little hand on my shoulder that fell into a cuddle.
I know it shouldn't be this way around, the comforting.
But in a day that felt so wrong I knew I had done something right.

Nothing like a cuddle from your toddler to bring the happy tears.

Mum Friends

We used to stand there talking to each other with our hips jutted forward, like an awkward teapot. Chatting about hospital bags with smiles that didn't belong to us.
I never knew I could talk for so long about a bag.
We were nervous.
But we hadn't said so yet.
In fact we weren't saying much at all for two women constantly chatting.
There was a lot of nodding.
And some weird disconnect.
Maybe because we thought growing humans was all we had in common.
Maybe because we were scared.
But we talked about the hospital bags some more.
Like it mattered.
And then somewhere after the hospital bags came the nappy bags and the cross over striped tops.
We were messaging over poo texture, catching up for play dates where we both just sat on the couch with babies attached, then would occasionally move to the floor to change a nappy.
We would find each other online at 2 in the morning, the little green dot of affirmation that I wasn't alone.
We would talk about the highs, we would cry over the lows.
We would laugh about how we thought birth would be the hardest part.
We understood the significance of the first roll over and the sadness of their last feed.
We'd remind each-other we were wonderful mothers on those harder days.

It's the only friendship where you get to know them later, who they were before they were a mum and I'm not talking about their job. It comes out in a Spotify playlist or in the clothes that follow the stretchy waistbands or the swear words that fall out of their mouth that you pleasantly welcome.

The friendship where you'll embrace them when they're upset before you know their dogs name.

Suddenly, you share so much more than a due date.

Three years on and we talk about a lot more than bags, but still the occasional, 'this handbag actually works as a nappy bag'.

And sometimes, for a few minutes we just sit in silence and watch the kids play.

Someone who I can sit in silence with and let out the longest breath.

Someone I never knew I needed.

Welcome Home

I remember when I brought you home 19 months ago with a bag of clothes you'd soon outgrow, moments between us you'd outgrow too.

I remind myself of this late at night, through the hallway tunnel, while I'm crossing the bridge made of your cries.

I become the unfaltering arch across where you lie, or the island that floats in stormy waters.

I wear your sleepy breath on my chest like armour. Yes I'm tired, but my protests of tending to your needs are tiring too.

I've been lost, I've ached and my heart has screamed with swinging feet that find the ground.
Your needs know not of inconvenient hours.
And love shines brightest in the dark.

I brought you home 19 months ago, and I will keep bringing you home every night that you need me.

You'll outgrow your clothes, you'll outgrow this phase and one day the nights will be filled of slumbers and restful hearts.
In some ways you'll outgrow me then too.

You won't remember this, but I hope you remember the light in the dark, the one you'll search for no matter how old you are.
Always welcoming you home.

I'm Sorry

It was one of those days, I had a pit in my stomach. I wasn't winning and the rainclouds were following me.

The lights were red. I was tense, my foot hard on the break.

'I just wanted to apologise for earlier', I started.
'I was wrong to yell, sometimes I lose my cool and it wasn't your fault…It wasn't your fault at all.'

I flicked up the window wipers as the weather got heavier.

'When you came through Holly's door to tell me about spilling your milk… it woke her. I was upset and I yelled. We were all tired, weren't we?'

Silence.

Apart from the murmur of traffic, all in our own little worlds, all on different journeys.
I wondered how many other apologies were currently being given to two year olds in cars right now.

'I made a mistake', I continued. 'I don't always get it right, I shouldn't have yelled at you, I feel really sad that I upset you.'

The wipers guided the splashes away as my sleeve did the same.
I turned around to him and held his hand, he squeezed mine back.
'I'm sorry', I said watching him.

He held on, his little fingers were so soft, I have to remember how little they are I thought.

I could see he was thinking.

'Mummy, it's okay', he said at last in his triumphant voice with those perfect inflections.

'I'll try better, promise'.

I hope he knows I mean it.

I turned back around, foot relaxing off the break as the lights turned green.

'Mummy?'

'Yes?'

'It's not sunny today, Mummy'.

'No darling, it's not'.

But I could see it peeking through.

Bouncing Back

I once told a woman not long postpartum that she'd really 'bounced back'. I had no children of my own then but she looked great and I thought it was what you said to new mothers.
It wasn't.

After my first pregnancy no one spoke those words to me. It was something I longed to hear. I was actually really proud of my body, I just didn't know I could be without being fit and toned. I wanted to smile at what I saw in the mirror.
I couldn't.

After my second pregnancy I suffered from postnatal anxiety, I drank a lot of coffee because I was up all night and I didn't eat a lot because I always felt full, of nerves mostly. The weight just fell off me. Later, I would find out about postnatal depletion.
I kept telling everyone, 'I'm fine, I'm fine'.
I wasn't.

I went out one evening with some friends and someone greeted me with, 'wow you've really bounced back'.
I thought about the previous night, my back to the wall at 2am breathing through the cries, my top in the car I had changed last minute because there was spew down it, the nipple cream on my bedside. I thought about the immense change we go through entering motherhood, how utterly fragile, yet strong we are.
I wondered why we considered 'going back' to be more beautiful than becoming, when it isn't.

I thought all along I needed to hear those words.
I didn't.

See You Soon

I held you long before my arms did, in my dreams and thoughts.
I whispered to you the lullabies that would later send you off to
sleep.

I knew you long before I met you, I would talk of your
personality made up of elbows and knees, 'ready to keep me on
my toes', I would say.

I loved you long before I saw you, tracing black and white prints
of your lips, knowing soon enough I'd be kissing them with my
own.

I heard you long before your cry into the world. That first
heartbeat, the one that echoed love and relief, a quick rhythm
that made time slow down.

I wanted you long before I needed you, as I sat there willing tests
to show me the lines that would change my life.

I felt you long before I touched you, the stretches of my belly
proudly growing you. The pain that sometimes comes with being
made of each other, the worry, that I couldn't be without you
now.

I shared with you my heart, before you'd steal it completely.
I've shared stories, ones of how I met your father, books already
sitting on your shelf. I've shared unspoken emotions with you
that I know you can feel.
I've shared my body, I am your land, and you are my guide.

When it's dark at night I wonder, will it be tonight?

I'm nervous
There's so much I don't know.
But I know I love you.
I'm ready
when you are.
See you soon,

love, Mum.

My Sensitive Boy

You're perfect you know, I often watch you and think that with tears in my eyes.
I'm also filled with anxiety upon leaving the house sometimes, a path of eggshells laid out for me.

You are a fire that spits, that cracks, that can burn out from a heart so big.
I don't always know what to do, sometimes I just sit and wait for you to calm down, wondering how I can be there for you both, when your needs are so different.
I don't want to contain you, I just want to help you.
I think back to you at 4 months old at the baby groups, I knew we were different.
I would wince at a balloon bobbing along waiting for the pop, waiting for you to be in hysterics, waiting for us to leave.
A motor bike or sirens up ahead.
A baby crying.
Someone unfamilar looking at you.
I held my breath a lot.

You are so loving, I know everyone can see it, but wow I see it like it's our secret.
If a sad melody comes on, tears will come and sometimes you ask me to turn the music off, sometimes you just sit with your head bowed and you listen and my heart breaks.
It's a gift but it's heavy, little one.

I'm unwrapping you to your core and I'm learning about me too.
Both of our unveiling.

You see things with fresh eyes, and you teach me to unlearn with mine.

I feel guilty when I breathe a sigh of relief when I drop you off at kindy. Yet I can't wait to pick you up.

I lose my patience a little when I turn the tap on to wash your hands and it's 'too fast' then 'too slow' then 'too fast', and we're late.

I feel awful when your hands find your ears because it's all too much and I realise sometimes it's my voice that's too loud.

I won't apologise, because I'm proud of you. The world needs more of you, yet I still worry and think of you before everything we do.

You radiate.
You question.
You absorb.
You FEEL.
And you're rocked by it.

I want to take the weight off you, but I can only take your hand.

I will continue to do better for you, my love.

To the parents of beautiful highly sensitive ones,
I know it comes with challenges.

I'm there with you, and I see you there for them.

For Some of Us

Loneliness is a clearing in a forest. But growth still happens there, the sun still shines through, and we're surrounded by the invitation of life.

My belonging was so obvious, and at the same time felt out of reach. If only I could tell myself back then, I was a part of something so big, so beautiful, I wasn't as small as I felt in those moments.

Without even realising, I was turning towards home, to the truest part within, the sun finding me through it all.

- Because it gets easier

Stop Complaining

Someone said to me once, you chose to have kids, don't complain'.

I thought, is that what I'm doing? Complaining?
By sharing how I feel?
Does that mean I'm just resigning myself to the fact I now hate motherhood?
I love my two more than anything, in fact love isn't a strong enough word.
It's just, not every day is sunshine and rainbows. We aren't wearing matching outfits with a day packed full of activities and not everyone's laughing all the time.

I had one particular day recently that hit hard. Forget all the 100 things I had to do, forget the fact that they were both screaming for me, forget the fact that food was thrown and I felt like a maid, that the couch was drawn on and we'd had a rough night. It wasn't even that.
I'd had some bad news over the phone and I just couldn't gather a thought in between it all.
The not getting a second to process or a chance to compartmentalise.
O V E R W H E L M.

I put down the phone, I had one of them at my leg whining, another one had a nappy accident, it was lunch time soon and I just couldn't process the news.
I didn't yell, or cry, in fact I just went really quiet and sat on the couch and stared blankly at the wall and allowed myself to just

feel a bit crap for a moment before tending to them.
That's what can be so hard, trying to help our little ones to process their emotions when we don't get a moment to process our own.
You don't stub your toe and say, 'hey at least I have toes'.
Or have a horrible day at work and not talk about it because well... at least you have a job.
Why should motherhood be any different? Without the guilt of saying at the end, 'but I wouldn't have it any other way'. Of course you wouldn't! You love those little guys!

Children's feelings don't need fixing, they need to be felt.
And so do ours, it's not all too different.
We all need a moment to just FEEL.
It's important to talk about the highs, it's just as important to talk about the lows.
That's not complaining- that's feeling.

Do You Let Him Cry?

'Do you ever just let him cry?'

I was 8 weeks postpartum and the nurse was over for her routine checkup.
my baby was tired so I put him down in his cot and I came back out so she could start asking me the questions from her clip board.

One question in and I heard cries from the room, so I excused myself and went to him. He was a magnet and my feet were moving.

I came back out with him, happy for him to nap on me so as not to keep her waiting and she asked me.
'Do you ever just let him cry?'

I remember this because it took me by surprise.
I responded with a hesitant, 'No', which sounded more like a question.
She looked a bit disapproving and I started to feel like I was failing all over again.

Almost 3 years on and another baby later, she could ask me how they're sleeping and I'd be honest. Some nights are great, some aren't. We didn't crack the 'sleep code', no.

But when I think back to those first few weeks postpartum, I can remember so many questions swirling around in my head.
Am I doing this right?

Am I enough?
Those questions were always put to rest when I went to him.

It's funny how the responsive approach tends to cop the most flak, but it gave my voice strength over a practice condemned as weak.

It hasn't been easy, there have been nights where we have all ended up in tears, usually as a result of me doubting myself, when I've closed the door on my heart and opened a book instead.

But the nights are more restful now and the girl all these years later wouldn't have that same timid and shaky voice.

For so long I doubted my need to reassure him.
I wonder how different things would be if the mother was reassured too.

It's Not Babysitting

When my husband goes grocery shopping with one of the kids, he's a star.

Seriously he could be on a stage with roses thrown at him because he's looking after them alone.

He comes home laughing (but flexing) telling me of the comments.
'Ohhh well done'.
'Ohhh so cute, good on you'.
'Isn't Mum lucky getting a break'.

Funnily enough, my grocery experiences aren't like that. Usually I get a wide berth and side eyes as I say on repeat,
'Almost done'.
'Don't touch that'.
'You can eat that soon'.
Definitely no adoring fans over here.

Once Drew and I were out walking with the kids, he had Holly in his arms while pushing an empty pram and some older man walked passed and laughed 'oh ya poor sod'. Meanwhile I was carrying two bags with the other flailing child.
'Hey mate, I'm a poor sod too', I wanted to say.
And news flash buddy...
Dads don't babysit, they parent.

Yes, these comments may be well meaning, they may seem encouraging, but at the end of the day, they're looking after their own children. Society still seems to have that lingering undercurrent that Dads are amazing if they share in the parenting.

I'll admit there's nothing better than an amazing Dad, but I won't be dishing out accolades for nappy changes.
I'm not 'lucky'
I'm grateful.
Very grateful for him.

Instead of, 'here's to the dads who baby wear, change nappies, get up in the night, cook meals or who simply show up'...

Here's to the Dads who say, 'I love you, I love us', by doing all of these things.

It's not just showing up as a father, it's showing up as a husband or partner too.

Redefining Beauty

I let myself grow through the weeds that whispered of what
petals should look like.
Wild at heart but soft to the touch.
Their thoughtless words of borrowed ideals.
Leaving blotches like hot showers.
What motherhood *should* look like.
What I *should* look like.
My body, a subject line.
While I look at my reflection and meet the new parts of myself.
Stories of raw courage at my core.
Sketches of happiness at my eyes.
Yes, I let myself go.
To wander and get wonderfully lost, so I could be found,
somewhere still where moments can breathe.
Where beauty isn't defined.
But I must radiate it every day.
Because I have never felt as beautiful since having you.

The Every Mum

The gentle mum, the yelly mum
The can I just be both? Mum

The tomorrow will be better mum
The just get through today mum

A bit of a helicopter, 'here, let me'
The risk taker, the adventurer
The just wait and see
The don't make me laugh or I might pee

The penny for your thoughts mum
The confident outspoken mum
You think you know her story mum
You don't, so just be kind mum

The dressing gown, the coffee in hand
The yoga pants, some self-care planned
Watch 'one born every minute', mum
The ignorance is bliss mum

I'm one and done, or what's two or five?
The only organic, or just eat to survive
The I need a moment alone mum
The cannot be without them mum

Crunchy, Yummy, whatever mum
Postpartum undies, saggy bum

2 years later cos' they're comfy, mum

The frazzled mum, the sweary mum
'I said truck, don't repeat that at kindy', mum

The 'I can rap this whole song in the car', mum
I got 99 problems... and baby shark is one

The larger body REAL mum
The skinny body REAL mum
The just stop talking about my body mum
Don't look at it, but what it's done!

The text book mum, the earthy mum
the I have no idea what I'm doing mum
The excuse the mess (but it's tidy) mum
The anxious, hovering, worried mum

The work out kind, the pay no mind
The mum tum, mum bun
5pm wine

The stay at home, the working mum
The both are hard on my heart mum
The crafty mum, 'let's whip up a cake'
The 'I'd rather poke out my eyes than bake'

But the thing is this,
you are good enough mum

If it's dark and restful, not a peep
Or if you're cuddling them whispering, 'go The f*** to sleep'

Because when the day is over and done
I'm a little bit of every mum.

Big Boys Don't Cry

I wonder how it must feel
to be a little boy
and hear things like,
'Big Boys don't cry'
when emotions come to you
as naturally as the air you breathe
will you one day choke on them
swallow them completely
into a bottle?
And I wonder,
as you grow into this big boy,
will your tears have dried?
the ones that were meant for loss
and happiness
and triumph
and beauty
and welcoming your child into this world
I wonder how you must feel
When for so long, you've been told not to
Now, a big boy
who's never felt
so little.

The Fourth Trimester

From the moment I saw you everything made sense, and nothing did.

I had no idea how terrifying love could be.

How could I never imagine life before someone I'd just met?

But still the tears would come. I was told to be grateful, as if I wasn't, it would be over before I knew it.

I waited for the weeks to swallow the days and the months to swallow the weeks until they were a pit in my stomach. I peeled guilt off gratitude for wishing moments away.

The days were still achingly beautiful though, I loved you all day long and even when blue, there was still you.

When you would wake my heart would do somersaults, I didn't have enough ointments to help, hot face cloths, cold gel pads. I wanted to feed you so badly, to look down and smile at you rather than straight ahead, rigid.

I started to accept the days of having nowhere to be, they stopped feeling like cancelled plans and I began to rest into it knowing in my heart, I wouldn't want to be anywhere else.

I would watch other mothers with their babies, I wondered if I would take you in my arms, predicting your movements like they did, opening myself up in the exact shape of your fall.

I didn't know that this was us already, that some things aren't learnt, some just are.

'I'm fine', I would say, always speaking for my future self.

As the sun would stretch its arms, I'd imagine the moon.

At night I sort of lay there with closed eyes in anticipation. Sleep trying to pull me down and my thoughts of you keeping me up.

Being a mother as well as a wife wasn't as easy as I thought, why did the two feel so separate like my skin could only belong to one?

Comments felt more like prods, 'how is he sleeping', 'oh, you're on formula now I see', 'you really should be doing this'. I wanted to unhook the words from under my ribs.

I felt everything so much more, maybe you do when you're shedding the girl of yesterday, maybe you're meant to. I was packing up and labelling boxes of myself and unpacking others, I was busy inside, changing and rearranging.

I felt like I had no right, because everything was so wonderful, how dare it rain inside when the sun was shining?

You were the best thing that ever happened to me, but frills don't always belong around the fabric of early motherhood. The fourth trimester was hard. I know it was hard for you too.

There's no way to describe it really.

The irony, that we couldn't have got through it without each other.

Oh Good, You're Home

"Oh, good you're home, it's not like I was waiting at the window or anything....

I've had a helluva day.

Oh that text at 5:02pm? Yea that was just me, don't worry, just thought something might have happened to you.

The hours between 4:30pm and 5:00pm really draaaaged.

It's been mental, I got the dinner on but there's dishes everywhere and I did clean but there's no point with these two, just look at the place. .. KID'S DADDYS HOME… Honestly I feel like the TV has been on all day... it hasn't... There's been a lot of tantrums today, I just don't know what's going on with him at the moment, could be a leap but I'm not sure, you know LEAPS? Remember I showed you that app that time? Ugh... Don't worry, just get the kids ready for dinner.

Oh by the way I made that appointment for tomorrow, you know the one… we talked about it a week ago.. you know, with the thing... HANG ON KID'S DINNERS COMING. Honestly I can't get a thing done around here, every time I'm on the way to do something I see something else that needs to be done, so this weekend we really need to get onto some things, I made a list. Looking after these two is a full time job you know …it's not easy, their naps were awful today so I had absolutely no time, NONE. Must be nice having a hot cup of coffee at your desk. Also that washing's still out there, I might need you to grab that later before it rains and the dog needs to go out.

I need a wine.

Come in the door would you.

Oh, how was your day?"

Reflection

I will never apologise for you,
make excuses or look down on you.
You aren't some ruin I need to fix,
or excess baggage I need to claim.
As you've evolved I have too.
This idea of beauty,
now magic skin.
Feeding on demand,
creating life,
rocking until I can no longer feel.
A selfless love that you have shown,
stretching to the stars,
with maps of our journey,
a now mutual address.
Sharing the spaces of you
and holding my hand.
Even when I haven't been so kind,
you didn't let go.
Throughout these years of carrying me,
through reflections of disapproval,
I'm finally smiling back.
Thank you for what you have given me.
To my body, and the skin I am in.

The Little Things

I'm beginning to notice things I didn't before
Like your tiny gumboots waiting at the door

Curious fingernails with dirt underneath
The way you say 'ahhhh' as I brush those small teeth

Your little frayed toothbrush, where once there were two
The light in your eyes as you discover something new

Tissues upon tissues for that button nose
Hanging mountains of washing of tiny clothes

Colours and mess as I watch you creating
Painting with food while the dog sits there waiting

Those wobbly thighs before you hit the floor
A cuddle and a kiss as you try once more

The content that I feel seeing your full round tum
The love that I have for that cushioned nappy bum

That perfect home, remembering clean
Realising now, this is a what a home means

My mind clouded daily with nursery songs
The sweetest sound I ever heard when you sing along

Alerting me to every car, truck and plane
On our walks in the morning, every day it's the same

The longest nights as I stroke your hair
Your eyes flutter closed just knowing I'm there

The way you find joy in the simplest of things
In every season and what it brings

Understanding sometimes these may feel like a chore
Will be my fondest memories when I don't have them anymore

Before the training wheels come off and those new teeth come through,
I'll revel in these moments, this version of you.

Motherhood is a Marathon

Motherhood is the marathon we didn't train for.
It's what we get up for, rain or shine, on broken sleep and an empty tank. It's running alongside others and holding out an umbrella on those harder days. It's jumping over obstacles and tripping and falling, it's getting back up on unsteady legs.

No matter the hurdles, we keep on running.

It's lifting weights side to side, back and forth until little eyes are closed. Carrying the load from yesterday and tomorrow, in our minds, in laundry baskets, in our hearts. It's wrestling nappy changes, prams in and out of cars, little feet into shoes. It's holding yourself up time and time again.

No matter how empty the barrel, we always find strength.

It's the cross-country swim I wasn't prepared for. It's diving headfirst into cold water and needing to come up for air. It's sinking with tired arms, exhaustion giving way to surrender. It's the busy nighttime routines, piles of dishes and cancelled plans. It's keeping them afloat while finding your stride.

No matter the conditions, we keep on swimming.

It's running a relay and wanting to pass the baton at 5pm. It's admitting you need a break and catching your breath.
It's letting the tears fall, from depletion, from relief, from an insurmountable love.

No matter how testing, we're in this together.

It's the coaching role I got promoted to with no experience. The game planner, the teacher. It's encouraging little spirits and lifting them up. It's nourishing little bodies, watching them take risks while we bite our lips. It's taking their hands in ours and helping them navigate this world, so one day they can do it without us.

No matter how many times we may lose, we're still winning.

Motherhood is the marathon that begins with our prize and a never-ending finish line.

We became athletes from 'ready, set, go', and we will keep going, for them.

No matter what.

Information Overload

I suppose the hardest thing
If you really must know
Wasn't the pregnancy or birth
But the information overload

The second they arrive
The paperwork begins
Charts, schedules, pamphlets
The birth of the admin

It will come at you in all forms
What you should do, what they need
While you're still wearing adult nappies
And working out how to feed

Yes there will be noise
To the things you don't 'adhere'
You'll forget you know them best
Instead, you will compare

You'll tentatively ask some questions
After night 3 you'll be in a state
You'll tell them of that sleepless night
They'll pipe up, 'just you wait'

You'll be told about the cues
About this, that and the other
Nodding while trying to transfer him
from one arm to the other

And while the lights are shining
On the experts and their peers
We begin to dim our own
When we've been doing this for years

Books, subscriptions, apps
While they're there to help
It seems that in the index
'Instinct' was left out

They'll talk of independence
A grown up word no less
Moulded to fit the narrative
That sleep is the only success

They'll speak about the regressions
And all their different cries
You'll google search the lot
Forgetting you have ears and eyes

Maybe now we're learning
This thing that sets us apart
Is leaning into ourselves
And trusting what's in our heart

And yes, I know it's hard
Worrying and not knowing
But each cry, each gaze, each single day
The both of you are growing

And while there will be suggestions
You'll get them on the daily
With the best intentions
And you'll listen to some, maybe
But please take a deep breath, Mama.
Because you've just had a baby.

Falling In Love

We'd sip on coffee in the kitchen, take out menus, playlists on repeat, his hand that slid into my back pocket.
Now, dust dancing around rolled up nappies that sit next to pots and pans as unfamiliar as we feel.
My belly, wild and willful now echoes primal groans.
My mind, as full as my bedside table with textbook spines much thinner than mine.
The nights of wine and laughter seem a distant memory.
My eyes, a river that welcome the shower.
My heart that bursts and twists and gives.
My hips swaying to the rhythm of all the lost slumbers.
My hands, fearful of not holding it all together.
My heart, a vehicle always travelling north.
And the kitchen, now full of noise, leg tugging and grumbling tummies.
Tasting from spoons before dinner is ready.
His hand welcome in my back pocket once more.
We fall in love all over again.

We fall in love all over again.

These Are the Moments

These are the moments I want to line my memory with.
The delicious double chins asleep in car seats.
The way the words, 'My Son', fell from my husband's lips like
they always belonged.
The first time my eldest translated for my youngest.
How she tucks her hair behind her ears.
How he pulls up his sleeves when he's hot, when did he work
out such a simple yet amazing thing?
That freckle.
The smell of their rooms.
How she used to feed and play with my hair.
His lashes.
When they sing a song.
My mind lingers here and not on the photos with numbered
cards.
But the arms of my memory can only hold so much.
These are the moments.

Don't let me forget.
Don't let me forget.
Don't let me forget.

Our Love Story

My favourite love story is ours, you tell it best.

You held my attention before we met.

I adored the ground you walked on before your first step.

I imagined up our future memories before any had been made.

I held you longer than my arms knew they could.

I rested into you,
you rested into me.

I stopped to take in the scenery again, and even through the
storms, it was beautiful.

Little things brought me joy, watching you.

Even dust swirling in the sunlight seemed like magic.

You slowed me down.
You gave me strength.
I gave you life,
and you gave me life back.

Our love story is the best I've heard.
You spoke to my heart,
before your first word.

When

I spent the early days wondering about the 'when'.
When will he crawl?
When will he walk?

Google searches had me concerned he wasn't crawling yet, and
then when he was, I averted my concerns to when he would be
walking. He was always much bigger for his age too, but here I
was thinking he would fit into some milestone box.

Always replacing a worry with a worry, how tiring.

I had subscribed to emails telling me what he 'should' be doing
or saying by certain ages and mostly it would just send me into a
much unneeded panic.

He was supposedly 'behind' in these milestones and yet I cannot
believe how fast he can run now and the beautiful little
conversations we have.

He was never 'behind', he was just doing things on his time, the
only time I needed to count on.

I realised after much anticipation for something to happen, how
final it was when it was over. After he walked, he never crawled
again.

Because the 'when' *will* come and the now will be gone.

The lessons we learn, always when it's too late.

Are You Having Any More?

I'm often asked if we'll have a third and usually, 'no way', rolls off my tongue. But if I'm honest, when I'm alone and the children are sleeping (of course), I do think about it.

Even though it's manic and my heads barely above water, I'm going to miss this imperfect season we're in.

Even though some days are incredibly hard and people will tell me, 'you got this', I don't always 'have this'.

Still, I get through, without it, but with us all intact.

Even though in the mornings I want to spend an hour in the shower washing the broken sleep off me, at night I linger in their warm sleepy breath as they drift off.

Even though I miss the girl my husband fell in love with, he says she's right here. It's just hard to see her through the old maternity bra and new lines round the eyes.

I'm finding her in fragments day by day.

Even though some days it feels like a tide I'm swimming against, still, it sweeps me up and leaves me breathless.

I didn't strut down the catwalk of motherhood like I thought I was going to. I felt pushed out, naked on stage in shoes I wasn't used to wearing. The beginning was tough, but I miss it.

It's beautiful and sometimes terrible, and they coexist together and somehow make perfect sense.
Even though it's falling down and getting back up, it's falling harder for them, every single day, over and over.

Maybe you never feel 'done' with a love like that?

Faces of Motherhood

There is the face of 2am, the silent hour filled with screaming. The pleading, and the gratitude of the breath on your neck that gives you your own.

The face of desperation, opening your heart but closing a door, just to breathe, just for a moment.

The face of helplessness, that inner child who wants to be seen, who needs to know she is doing OK.

The face of exhaustion, the forced smiles, the glazing over eyes, the hand that finds the remote. Just watch this for a little bit, then reheats coffee.

The face of nostalgia, the simultaneous pull of looking forward and looking back. Holding on and letting go.

The face of adoration, the high-pitched excitement that lies in the little things, as they teach us, to remember.

The face of defeat, the sleeve caught on the door handle, the tears in the car, the last straw. That mother who holds it all together to let it all out.

The face of guilt, I don't get you, what is going on with you, I love you but I don't like you right now. I know this is hard for you, this is hard for me too.

The face of worry, of the things we wish we could undo and things not yet done. Like a homesick feeling that lives inside your head.

The face of pride, a galloping heart that is concurrently still, an overwhelming feeling of wanting to make the world a better place, for them.

The face of empathy, the pain you feel as if it were yours. The only pain you've ever wanted to make your own if it meant protecting them.

There are so many faces to motherhood.

But through the tears, the struggles and the moments we break, is that unbreakable love.

Because that's what makes it worth it.

In the face of it all.

You're Not Lost

Today I felt lost.
My head was throbbing from the rough night before and the day turned into chaos.

I had them both tugging at each leg while I was trying to get lunch ready, one crying and overtired, the other I didn't really know why.

There was just so much needing me.
So, so much needing.
Even the cat was howling at me.
The washing was beeping.
The fridge door was beeping.
Must everything beep?
And screech?
And touch me?
It all felt too much.
Between life admin and a day of losing, I just fell to pieces on the kitchen floor.

I was pushed and pulled in so many different directions that I broke.

I just broke.

I didn't want to wear my brave face in that moment.

So I didn't.

Then two soft voices said 'mummy',
My heart and soul,
and I wondered how that word could ever make me want to tear my hair out, but moments ago it did.

I just wanted to be alone.

So when my husband got home that evening I marched my dinner into the bedroom and sat there on the bed.
I could still hear them calling for me and I just shut my eyes.

Then the whole house softened a little and I took a breath.

Some days are heavy, really heavy.
But I realised, this was my dream, it really was.
Everything we had hoped for we had.

Them.

Even through the mess and tears and the days we had to squeeze each other's hands a little tighter.
It wasn't perfect but who said it was meant to be.

So, I took my half-eaten plate back out to the dining room and sat down with my family.
And just like that, all is forgiven.

I'm always filled with gratitude, but some days make me wonder who I am.
And if I'm honest I don't really know now without them.

But as they say,
'You're not lost,
You're here'.

Not 'Just'

You are not 'just' anything
Not just a woman
Or just a friend
A wife
A partner
Or just a mother
You are a universe
Made up of waves that brought life
Stars that hold dreams
Landscapes of home
Rocks that will crumble but will always remain
The winds gentle sway, and strongest roar
You are someone's 'all'
And 'all' is not lost
You are a mother
But never, just.

With You

Oh, how there are a million things to do
And I'll do them, I will
I'll do those too
But right now
I'll just be,
Here,
With you.

Oh, how I want to sleep, I do
And one day, I will
I'll sleep right through
But right now
I'll just be,
Here,
With you.

Oh, how the days are long, it's true
Yesterdays are many
But todays are few
So I'll fill them up
With all of you
And simply be,
Here,
With you.

Start As You Mean To Go On

'Start as you mean to go on'.

I read that quote across many parenting books, ones that would make me think that somehow, I would go into motherhood knowing exactly how I was going to parent from the get go, that I would know exactly what I was doing and all would be fine if we started something the "right way", whatever that was.
But the notion we will start something and stick to it means we aren't learning and evolving with them.

I've learnt so much from them already.

How beautiful their world is when I surrender into theirs instead of pulling them into mine.

How this age won't keep, but the memories will when I slow down, just a little.

How I don't need to be the perfect mum with perfect lunchboxes and perfect rooms styled with a Pinterest paintbrush. While I appreciate a beautifully styled room, they don't.

How I won't spoil them by going to them when they need me. How 'rods' and 'habits' should be replaced with words such as 'instinct' and 'trust'.

How resilient mothers are. I've been knocked down in the throes of motherhood many times, but I get back up. Some days I feel as if I'm made of glass but it's that unbreakable love that holds me together.

How all this 'dependence' and this 'picking them up', will one day become independence anyway and my arms will be empty and so will their rooms. But I hope they'll still fall into my arms when they need me, no matter their age.

I started with shaky steps out of the hospital, my mind full of worries and my body slightly numb.
How was I allowed to leave with this baby?
What if I didn't get it right.?
What about all those habits?
And all those rods?

Today we can barely make out the start line when we look back.
And you won't look back.
Start as you mean to.
Go on.

All Of It

Imagine all the things we didn't have to do, like the dishes and the washing and cleaning up after tiny humans, rushing around to quickly wipe hands before they find the couch.
Wouldn't it be nice to be present and push those things aside and be in the moment.

BE IN THE MOMENT.

I'll admit, I find that so hard.

I still have this NEED to tick things off a list to feel as if I've achieved something, yet at the end of the day when I'm lying in bed it's not the chores I got done that make me smile.
And I know this and yet...
I still get so frustrated with them when I can't get to them, as if they're keeping me from my chores, like THEY are a chore.
Oh and the guilt from that!

It's hard when one job becomes two then suddenly ten and all of a sudden you realise you'll only ever chase your tail until tomorrow where you'll do it all over again.

It's no trade off though is it? I mean, it all seems so petty when the reward is having children. But the things that made you tick before babies are all of a sudden replaced and regardless that takes some getting used to.

They make me tick.
But I need to do things for me too.

And it's hard to accept that sometimes those things are
just getting the washing on the line, the new norm!

I had two little innocent faces looking at me today when I broke
down at smeared egg all through our shaggy rug, it's beyond
saving.
I think I'll throw it out.
I liked that rug.

I don't want to be too exhausted for play, or pick up my phone
to escape for a moment or sigh at another "mummyyyy" when
I'm trying to go to the toilet.
But I am today, because some days are just hard.

It's the hardest job in the world, because it's the most rewarding
job in the world, because it doesn't always feel like that, even
though you know it is, even though you'd have it no other way,
even though you'd kill for a moment alone, even though you
can't be without them.

It's hard, it's lonely, it's beautiful, it's messy.

It's exhausting.

All of it.

Can You Tell Her?

In those small hours of the night
Do you see her?
As she pulls on her robe, guided by the sound of aching cries.

As the waves of defeat rise
Can you hear her?
When all is silent apart from the sound of her breaking heart.

When her arms feel heavy
Do you think of her?
As she sways and soothes to the rhythm of two hearts beating.

When she looks in the mirror
Do you know her?
As she stares back, desperately, searching for pieces of the
woman she once knew.

When time stands still
Can you stand with her?
Nobody told her of a love like this and how it would leave her
breathless.

When she reaches for them
Did you notice her?
How beautiful she looks, a natural, even if she doesn't realise it.

When she was born
Did you hold her?

While she gazes at the rise and fall of a chest that breathes life into hers.

And as she counts up the stars, she wonders
If she is enough.
Can you tell her?
That she is.

She is a mother.
We are mothers.
And we are incredible.

Sunday

Sundays are no longer
days of the week
but rather,
moments
wrapped in each other
where your head
finds my shoulder
and I try to forget
all those things 'to do'
for just a moment and lay here
with you
in this moment on Monday
my lazy Sunday.

My Shooting Star

Sweetheart, how I've searched
For a shooting star
To wish away the nights
Where sleep feels oh so far

I feel as if I'm fading
But I can hear you call
My heavy heart beats faster
As love comes stumbling down the hall

Is she a good baby?
Still echoes in my mind
Yes you are I'll tell them
For the comfort in me you find

I know these nights are numbered
Your eyes they flutter closed
We envelop together
As you begin to softly doze

They tell me I should leave you
Just wait until tomorrow
But this journey won't be ours.
When advice is simply borrowed

It won't be forever
But my forever you will be
So we'll cover up in moonlight
Before it cradles you without me

And when the tunnel fades
When the light begins to shine
Your little head won't rest on me
And we'll sleep through the night

But right now in the dark
Though I long for sleep
The chapters in these moments
Is the only book I need

I look out to the sky
Then I look down at you
I don't need a shooting star
To make a wish come true.

The Good Old Days

Now that you're a mother
They say that you will change
And what a gift it is
To never be the same
To take with you the old
And rearrange the new
To hold a little hand
That grows alongside you
You'll hope you don't forget
You'll try to remember 'then'
You'll drift back to the 'good old days'
Seeing now, that this, was them.

Head Full of Questions

Some nights as I'm stroking your head, mines full of questions, heart full of blame.

I didn't play with you enough today, I should have, but I was drowning in things that I had to get done.

I should have prepared more activities for you, read you more books, was the TV on for too long?

Did I yell too much? I really hope you remember the cuddles and laughter over the yelling.
Heart now full of apologies.

I say 'No' a lot, maybe too much? 'Mummy can't right now', I say that a lot too.

I'm here, you're here, my mind sometimes elsewhere.

After a really hard day I told my husband I had 'checked out', I didn't mean it, but I was trying to shorten 'I'm so tired, I'm at breaking point and I need a moment'.

It didn't need to be shortened.

And so the little seeds of doubt grow into full bloom as I'm feeding them the, 'Did I give you enough?' questions.

I think of what I know to be true.

There is no place I'd rather be than here, even if I don't feel that way every second of every day.

Driving the long way home doesn't dull the light in my eyes when I see you.

You're my thought before everything I do, but never an afterthought.

I smile just at the thought of you, even in my dreams.

And despite all my questions, my immeasurable love for you is not one of them.

As you drift off, my lingering thought,
I hope you always know that.

This Mother Love

I am as sharp as I am soft, and so is this mother love.

Sometimes it's so intense, it pierces me deeply and I bruise and bleed over worst case scenarios, over the worry of loss.

Sometimes it's calm, a rounded feeling, as if my life had a backing track with notes that make me weep,
untethered, unexplainable.

My pause button is the plastic box of baby clothes in the garage.
Maybe we'll give them to their kids one day.
Or maybe I'll pull out the size one green and blue striped tee shirt when the house is silent. The one that makes me think of sunblock, and his first summer.

It's harsh and it's quiet. It woke me up inside and still I'm dreaming. Some days I'm floating, and others I'm thrashing in the waves.

It's the easiest feeling and the hardest lessons. It's the itch inside a bone, it's something even reason cannot know.

It's as long as the nights that bring you to your knees, and as clear as the phantom cries in the shower.

It's emotions that leave flesh wounds and heal you all at once.
A wild belonging, this mother love.

I Remember

I forget sometimes we had a life before them, there's evidence of it of course. In photos, in conversations, in a glance of appreciation. But if it weren't for the life we had before, I wonder what our life would be like now.

I remember the nights out, drinks flowing, loud music, dancing, laughing in taxis on the way home.
Then the nights became broken, accompanied by my tears and lots of shushing. Your hand never far and mine never far from pushing it away. We still danced, like idiots around each other flustered, trying to prepare bottles, find a thermometer or a burp cloth.

I remember you breaking down my walls, only for me to build them back up. I've said things I don't mean just to watch you feel something.
And as I slowly let the pieces of me down, I wondered if I was still the same girl you fell in love with.

I remember happily listening to your work stories and now you'll get home and I appreciate you don't linger in the car beforehand. I sometimes wonder what it must feel like to walk in the door to our manic ways. I was never there to greet you with a kiss. I wanted to, but instead some chore would take its marks on my tongue.

I remember knowing each other's every little detail and now I'll tell you something a week later that I simply forgot about, but I'll still text you during the day, especially when it's been hard.

Sometimes I type something out and then delete it, like I just need to know you're there.

I remember closing the door to the toilet and now it's everyone's favourite meeting place. I'm asking you to grab my postpartum undies out of the draw and you know the ones. I used to think we were comfortable with each other, now I know we are, on a whole new level.

I remember flutters, when you'd wear a suit, the back of your neck, the first time you looked at your child.
Those flutters are a peaceful kind now. I'm moved the most when time stands still.

I remember talking about our dreams, this was one of them, we just didn't know it then and how perfectly imperfect it would be.

And somewhere between a bedside of ointments and our kids playing in the yard, there became a sudden ease.

Our conversations weren't so compulsory, and we were laughing more. We started finding time for ourselves and I started kissing you as you walked through the door again.

There's no one I'd rather compare eye wrinkles with and be exhausted with.

No one I'd rather smile with across the room of chaos.

Some days stretch on forever, but there's no one I'd rather spend forever with.
Look at this life we have.

This was our vision, yet we never saw it coming.

Almost Two

You're almost two
And I'm in two minds
Of this twofold approach
Leaving me in all kinds

'She's growing up'
Better play by the rules
You're almost two
Should enrol you in school

That two step toddle
Better get ready
To see it in strides
As you become steady

You're almost two
You're practically grown
Two birds of a feather
Before you have flown

Is it all too much?
Being almost two?
You're 'terrible' now
And should know what to do

No longer a baby
Independence, you've plenty
Off on your way
Two going on twenty

You're almost two
I'll admit 'defeat'
For meeting your needs
On this two-way street

Cuddles before bed?
Don't give two straws
One stone, two birds
Cuddling you is no chore

'She's almost two'
'She's getting too old'
But my arms will lift you
As long as they hold

Here's a thing or two,
Why grow up so fast?
My heart is in two
Knowing this won't last

I'm in no rush
We're two of a kind
So here's my two cents
I'll pay no mind

Two heads, as they say
Is better than one
So let's lay them down
When the day is done

Let's write our own manual
I'll just enjoy you
Cos' you're pretty small
After all, you're just two.

What Are Friendship Goals?

Maybe it's not about the Mum Squad hashtags,
having a huge invite list or social calendar.
Maybe it's about counting the good friends on one hand, the
vulnerable messages in the quiet of the night, the ones who share
in the details of your life.
When the rain falls, they hold out an umbrella and weather your
storm. You've talked about growing old together, shared
laughter, secrets, and tears.
Fancy lunch dates can be snacks at home, and screens don't need
to come out to document your time.
It's the holding steaming mugs, sitting outside and watching the
kids play - It's a love found in the ordinary.
In the texts that follow straight after you've spoken.
The ones who line your soul.
Maybe this is enough.
Because life gets busy, and you only need two hands to hold a
few hearts close.

I Was Told

I was told my world would change.

I was told my house would change.

I was told I wouldn't sleep.

I was told I'd lose my sanity and myself.

I was told my body would change

And so would my bank balance.

I was told my life would change.

But they forgot to tell me I would change.

And I did.

In the best way.

Because of you.

Maybe they were saving the best for last.

How You Feed

I wanted the skin to skin breakfast in bed, lost in sheets and each-other's eyes.
I wanted the gazing the bond and the nourishing.
I wanted to succeed, to say I could, to comfort cries.
I wanted the lazy slumbers, the cuddles, the midnight hour tiny hands on my chin.
The touching of hair.
The sound of little breaths glugging, peace and eyes closed to a milk drunk surrender.
I wanted the thriving, healthy, happy baby.
I wanted them to look at me like I was their world, because they were mine.
I wanted to feed my baby.
I breastfed one to 14 months.
I bottle fed one after 2 weeks.
I think of both my journeys when I read this.
Though neither ending was easy on my heart, despite it now being so full.

Don't dim your light no matter how you feed, your light shines so bright to your baby.

Motherhood Is Not All of Me

I put all of me into motherhood,
But motherhood is not all of me.

Yes they complete me, though I was never empty.
Yes I do it for them, but I do things for me too.
Yes they make me happier than I've ever been, but I remember
the things that used to make me laugh, and they still do, though I
forgot for a while.

Postpartum felt rather long for me with two back to back,
it took a while to emerge.
It's funny how your heart can shatter and expand in equal
measure watching them grow, but this is how it's meant to be,
and if I'm honest, I'm a better mother now that I feel more me.

I remember going to my Mums netball games as a young girl, I
would sit and watch her on the stands, see how happy it made
her. I remember how it made me feel happy too.

It's important they see the me before mum. She may have
changed a little, but she's there, and she matters.
They'll always know I live for them, but not in the way that
sounds, that's a real weight to bear. I'd do anything for them, but
I want them to see me living for me, so that one day they'll do
the same.
So yes, I can say they're my every breath while needing a moment
alone to breathe too.

I can say I put all of me into motherhood,
but motherhood is not all of me.

Salt In the Sleep Deprived Wounds

Most nights as I get into bed I turn off my bedside lamp and lie there, not asleep nor awake... knowing I'll be up soon.
The last week my spot has been on the floor next to my daughter's cot and there has been swearing, tears, furiously checking leap apps and a whole lot of throwing back the covers.

Sleep around here is a novelty. If by some miracle chance they both sleep through it's always the first thing we talk about in the morning. Like, 'WOW, that was a good night', 'how do you feel'? As if we just won lotto or something, I imagine the feeling would be comparable.
Then we try and retrace what we did as if we had any real control over it.

But that's not usually the case, usually it's up at the butt crack of dawn dreaming of having a solid dream... Silver lining, coffee never tasted better on those mornings.

While I know one day this will all be a distant memory it doesn't make it any easier at the time. Not when you know what's ahead of you for the day and sometimes just the thought of it is enough to want the ground to open up and swallow you.
Also why do they always look so fresh in the morning?
Isn't that just salt in the sleep deprived wounds?

Despite 'tired', being my answer to, 'how are you?' I decided to stop worrying about the books and the noise about what I SHOULD be doing to have her sleep through long ago.

The more I read those the less I read her and intuition can't be found on a page.

Don't get me wrong, I've also had some amazing advice, but this is us here, it's where we end up, regardless.

Through all the books and articles in the early days I've realised that parenting isn't some formula you need to 'crack', It's a constant equation and a lot of head scratching, but a forever multiplying heart, one I can lead and love with when I listen to it.

I'll never forget these sleepless nights and how drained I feel, but I feel a sense of comfort knowing my presence makes her feel safe.
She's so small and new after all.

There will be people in her life that won't show up for her.
I don't want to be the first.

She won't have memories of these nights, no. But the feeling of me being there, I hope in some way she remembers that forever.

One To Two

You were all I knew,
before one became two.
You weren't my tiny baby anymore,
even though, a baby you were.
Just us, no longer.
No longer just us.
And when you both cried, I would cry too.
My first home, my first teacher.

The bigger you felt in my arms, the heavier my heart.
People would come over,
'Have some time with the baby', they would say.
And they would take my baby away.

I felt I needed to pull over and ask for directions, the
neighborhood was familiar but the street names had changed and
I wanted to find my way back to you.

Then, you took her tiny hand in yours and I realised what I had
given you, what I had given us.
Nothing felt harder,
but nothing was easier than loving you both.

There were days I couldn't divide myself,
where I'd fantasise of splitting myself in two.
but please know,
you walk around with my heart, as does she.
So in some ways, I'll always be
in two places at once.

Dear Husband (our little hour)

We don't have a lot of time for just us,
but we have our little hour.
Between 8 and 9.
Sometimes it's less, sometimes it's more.
It all becomes silent, apart from the humming fridge.
Or the dishes screaming at us.
Or our bed that calls for sleep.
I know the day is a freight train through our brains and our eyes
are tired.
And our love is quiet.
I don't need all the things,
Like flowers, or jewellery.
Just how you look at me in my dressing gown,
that really needs a wash.
Or the last piece of chocolate.
Or how you seem so taken when I tell you, 'I love you'.
Like it's the first time you've heard it.
Like you see me.
Like I see you and not all the tasks I need you to do.
While the extension of our love rests down the hallway,
let's cuddle up.
Let's not decide on a movie.
Let's say everything
And nothing.
Until one of us yawns.
Until one of them needs us.
Let's just be us.
The old and the new.
For our little hour.

My Favourite

People sometimes ask of my favourite days,
and I think of you being placed in my arms.
So small and new with those perfect wrinkles.
Those little cries I didn't yet recognise.
At times I needed holding too,
but oh, how I loved holding you.
Never had I felt so complete on empty.
Those slow-motion days now harder to glimpse.
You are the sun to my rise,
as I think back to my favourite days.

And then I wasn't supporting your neck anymore,
you were bouncing round on my hip instead.
Suddenly you were crawling and so was I,
discovering your new view with you
and all you would get into.
You wore your personality with pride
and as your confidence grew so did mine.
My heart was open and you filled it up.
You are the softness to my edges,
As I think back to my favourite days.

And then you were standing,
and I was standing a little taller too.
Growing into myself with you.
You were the chaos that gave me life.
As you took your first wobbly step you looked at me.
'Is This OK'? you asked with your eyes.
'It's OK' I nodded back.

And off you went.
I'd do anything for you.
You are the piece to my puzzle.
As I think back to my favourite days.

And now you're growing into those bloated cheeks,
a little boy before my eyes.
I think of the way your hand fits in mine.
The way you say, "I love you Mummy".
You are the beat to my heart.
We're lying on your bedroom floor and you're soaring your toy car in the air.
'It's REALLY fast Mummy, it's my favourite car'.
I look at you and tell you it's my favourite too.

My absolute favourite.

The Paradox of Motherhood

You can mourn the girl you were
and love who you are now,
You can build a beautiful life around
the days that come crashing down.

You can feel the sunlight on your face
from the bottom of the ocean,
You can watch your world as it stands still,
and never more in motion.

You can know where you are going
when your alignment's slowly shifting,
You can gasp under the waves,
or they can hold you while you're drifting.

You can trace their face for hours
until they fall asleep,
You can whisper that you'll remember it all,
a promise you may not keep.

You can be their universe
move mountains with a touch,
You can feel scared for no other reason
than you love them, so very much.

You can wish away the loneliness
when the nights are coffee black,
You can study the landscape of their skin
and look forward, while looking back.

You can feel closer to your partner
though the ground beneath you is shaking,
You can never be more tired
while something within you is waking.

You can exhale the hardest days
while you're still holding your breath,
You can give yourself over and over
when it feels like there's nothing left.

You can learn the art of holding on
while also letting go,
You can have no idea what you are doing,
even though deep down you know.

You can linger back to before you loved them
a time ago that felt so long,
You can hold that tiny hand in yours,
and never feel so strong.

You can take with you the old
while weaving in the new,
You can pick your tired bones up
asking, why nobody told you?

You can watch them like you've known them
forever and a day,
You can rest assured you have,
as it was meant to be this way.

You can be entangled,
beginning, middle, end,
You can wonder where your place is
knowing simply, it is them.

It's only confusing when you think
it's one without the other,
Because opposites can grow in gardens,
within you as a mother.

And make no sense and complete sense
and turn you inside out,
And love can hold you - *and it will,*
through all the tears and doubt.

Because motherhood is fast and slow
it broke and made me whole,
A divide that only multiplies
within your heart and soul.

Printed in Great Britain
by Amazon

f2711be5-c79b-491f-961f-4b4b9d5d0bffR01